Poems About You

PRAISE FOR POEMS ABOUT YOU

"... searingly personal and raw ..."

"At times sexy, at others emotionally heavy, Poems About You delivers an expressive, accessible collection of poetry perfect for those falling in love — and falling out of it.

With creative poem titles and highlights like "Maybe If I'd Worn Jeans, It Would Have Been Different" and "I'm Not the Fisherman's Wife," this book reads like a conversation between friends. Ellen excels at capturing the emotion of each piece.

[This collection is] searingly personal and raw ... well paced and clearly written for fans of all types of poetry."

– K. Provost
Writer and Editor

"... a beautiful message of genuine connection ..."

"In this collection are poems depicting scenes and themes about love. First love, falling in love, losing love, and connecting with others. It's about romance — the beautiful kind, the ugly kind and everything in between.

What Brynn captured here so beautifully were moments. It's the moments that make up a feeling or an emotion or a memory. Whether it's the feeling of a lover's touch or the weight of the words they say or don't. The thoughts we filter or don't. The way we show our love and accept it from others .... I loved the snapshot of memories here. Some are so raw and honest, others are whimsical and deeply funny.

The best poets know how to reach down deep and pluck out the messy bits, stitch them together and present them to us. And at its best, poetry has the power to heal and connect and make us feel, deeply, all the things. And Brynn has done that with her debut collection. I laughed. I teared up. It transported me to moments in my past with people I used to know. It's a beautiful message of genuine connection. I cannot wait to see what she releases next.

As the author notes: If you've ever loved or been loved ... these poems are for and about you."

– Christopher M. Tantillo
Author

TINY NEWT PRESS
BUFFALO, NY

Poems About You

Cover art by Brynn Ellen Semeraro.
Prepared for publication by Tiny Newt Press, LLC.

ISBN 979-8-9869335-2-8

eBook ISBN 979-8-9869335-3-5

Published by Tiny Newt Press, LLC
Buffalo, New York
www.tinynewtpress.org

CONTENTS

For the people who love me best
... and the ones who didn't

special thanks to:
DM, CT, TR, CD, SW, EM, KD,
AF, JS, DS, JH, DG, KS, OS, NG

my first readers, biggest supporters and inspirations

Selected poems from 2022 and 2023
Brynn Ellen Semeraro
@brynnellen_poet

A Note from the Poet:

I woke up on my 36th birthday suddenly very aware of my age, what I had accomplished thus far and what dreams and goals I'd been deferring. I wrote a poem in a word memo on my phone before I even got out of bed; I crafted a poem around that spark and with it a mission for my year. I committed to writing at least one poem a day for 365 days, promising a library of nearly 400 poems by my next birthday. There were no other expectations, no end goal ... just a bank of poems as a sort of journal to my 37th year as a human and an opportunity to stretch and grow a muscle that I had largely let atrophy since my creative writing classes in college.

In the time that has passed since that fated morning, I have written some 600+ poems. In the beginning, it was sometimes a chore; however, three or four months in, I was becoming so prolific that I often pumped out over a dozen poems a week. After my subsequent birthday, I gently allowed myself to slow down again ... but the muscle had grown strong and poems continued to begin writing themselves in my brain almost daily.

Over the course of this project, I learned a lot about myself. I experienced love, heartbreak, made new friends and lost some, changed careers, began to travel a bit, grew intellectually and shrunk physically, and consumed more coffee than a human probably ought to. I wrote poems about it all.

When curating this collection, I selected poems in which I was navigating romantic relationships with others. So much of what I went through this time period was orbiting around that theme. Though I have beautiful pieces about my children, nature, friends, myself and more, I really felt my strongest suit was to lead with the poems selected here.

If you've ever loved or been loved, these are Poems About You.

Poems About You

by Brynn Ellen

TINY NEWT PRESS
BUFFALO, NY

I take off my daily mask
When I walk through the door
The one I wear everywhere but here
There's no need to pretend with you
So I drop it to the floor
A few minutes of talking
Or one really good hug
Is enough encouragement
To lose my next layer of defense
I shrug it off like a heavy jacket
And giving up the extra weight
Is freeing and emboldening
My words come easier
And I'm suddenly babbling
About my dreams and wishes
And pulling you along with me
As I slide out of societal shoes too tight
A glass of wine or some home-cooked food
Helped to loosen
And gain brave barefoot traction
And by the time we're snuggled
Side by side on the couch
Piles of metaphorical laundry are heaped
And discarded all around me
Because you let me be comfortable
Stripped to my skin

"Bare"

It's your eyes
The green-leaning hazel
And the way they
Smile at me
In the tenderest way
When you tell me
You love me
It's the way they
Sparkle with mischief
And the tilt of your brow
As you embody
Alter egos that dissolve me
To childlike giggles
It's their depth
When you get real
And give voice to your worries
And limitations
The way they brim
And spill
When you're vulnerable
Or truly moved
It's the way they
Really see me
And the rest of the world too
As spaces of possibility
Beyond what others perceive
And the way they
Do all of this
Yet still arrest me
With their beauty

"That Shirt Brings Out the Green in Your Eyes"

One of your sexiest features
Is definitely your hands
And I know you think
That is just crazy
But have you ever watched
The way you use them
Deftly, purposefully, gently
With easy flow and grace
My own hands are awkward
They flit and fidget
Sweat and stress
My hands are prat-falling comedians
And yours are serious actors
I'm drawn into the story they're telling
In everyday actions
Or when they rest languidly
Or heaven help me, if they're touching me
Softly at my knee
Warmly at my back
Worshipfully at my face
Tenderly at my sides
Adoringly, artfully, painstakingly perfect
Those beautiful hands
But the best part
Is when I slip my hand in yours
And your hand gently squeezes mine
And my hands calm
And that calm spreads through me
I feel your love come from your hands
And there's nothing sexier than that

"Your Hands"

Today, instead of doing work
Or reading my book as I planned
I did something a little bit crazy
But it helped me to understand
I scrolled back and read every one of our texts
Every conversation we've had
I started at the beginning
And I know it might seem a bit mad
Like an old-timey widow
With boxes of letters from lovers long passed
I read our love back into newness
Tapped back into what would make it last
It's easy sometimes in the daily grind
To forget about the little ways we fell
The things we first found captivating
The first few times our heart swelled
In reading the lines, I got emotional
And remembered details about those first days
How clearly, in retrospect, we were both smitten
And showing it in little ways
Ways that I know so well now
I'm afraid I may take them for granted
I'm glad I took this chance to reopen my eyes
Remember what got me enchanted
I strive to hold on to this feeling
Fall in love with you again and again, forever
We have stored in our phones history
The love letters we wrote together

"I Have a New Favorite Author"

He looks a little like you
Is the first thought I have upon waking
Looking at my lover in bed
And thinking about you
A man I fell in love with
Nearly two decades ago
The man who broke my heart
Only a few years later
Once considered, the comparisons flood
And I'm tasting your name
When it's his in my mouth
And wondering where we went wrong
So I can keep that similarity at bay
Because if loving you and losing you
Nearly wrecked me then
And this is the universe gifting me
A chance to get it right
I'm gonna take it on with gusto
But if the shadow of recognition
Was a harbinger of things to come
I'm burying my head and my heart in the sand
He looks a little like you
But that maybe doesn't have to mean anything
Other than I have a type
And men I love are beautiful to me

"A Memory Muddles Reality"

I let myself be molded
Into you, number two
Because he loved you first
But I wanted him to love me more
I wanted to be the one
But now I'm just a shadow of you
And a fraction of me
And a hint of another love he still carries
Which is sad for all of us
Because you were better at being you
And I've forever lost a piece of me
She wasn't even what he pretended she was to him
And he was never satisfied with any of us anyway

"In His Wake"

My lips find your back
Even with closed eyes
My fingers trace paths
From your shoulders to thighs
As far as I can reach
I touch and awaken
'Til you've had just as much
As can be taken
You roll toward me enough
That my hands have new zones
They can softly explore
As you let out a groan
You're already hard
When I finally acquiesce
And touch you directly
Where — yes, I confess
My fingers and mind
Were eagerly itching to be
You sigh as I do
And press back against me
How long can I tease you
How long can I just touch
When I crave you inside me
God, I want you so much

"When I Wake Up Next to You"

Our dreams
Are haunted
By the inconsistencies
In what you want
And what I want
Because the Venn diagram
Overlaps enough
To make us see
A shared future
But the full scope
Shows a different story
In which less than a quarter
Of our dreams
Share the same space
And is that wedge
Enough to build in
Or can we both
Take on a little more
Of each other's dreams
And push those walls out
So we have enough
Space to grow
And keep dreaming
Together

"Pushing Out the Curved Walls"

If tomorrow I didn't wake up
Would this have been enough
To keep me in your heart
Until your days came to an end too

Or would it feel like wasted time
Left with unfulfilled promises
And just another bump in the road
Another failed attempt at having it all

Or would it be a relief of sorts
And a clean fresh start
To reinvent yourself again
Without the baggage of broken hearts

If tomorrow I didn't wake up
Would you try your hand at compromising
With an unbending God
Or maybe an unaffected Devil

Or would you simply accept
That life is unfair sometimes
And death has a way
Of leveling a senseless playing field

Or would you never be content again
Let my ghost haunt your heart
In the same way all your living lost do
And never learn to settle down and rest

"What Happens Next"

Sometimes you court chaos
Because it feels more active
More alive
You trick yourself into believing
Progress can only be made
If you're uncomfortable
And chaos isn't comfortable
And being comfortable
Is the worst thing you can imagine being
So you lean in to the wild
The chaotic, the haphazard
You tell yourself
This is really living
And vitality comes from adrenaline
Spurred by dopamine hits
And endorphin rushes
When what your brain really craves
Is some stabilizing serotonin
In regular, reliable quantities
But that is too hard
Or maybe too easy
Or maybe both

(continued -->)

Because you seek the only comfort
That you can trust
Believe in
Because you can measure the results
And the chaos lies to you
Calls it living
Calls it growing
Calls it getting comfortable with being uncomfortable
And throws into sharp relief
The other places where you're comfortable
Too comfortable, it mocks
And makes you question those things
And throw them into chaos too
It's killing your spirit
And making your body dig the grave
While it just keeps whispering
This is living
This is living
This is living

"Giving Chaos Power of Attorney"

When you say you need space
I don't hear a space bar click
And see the chasm between
A 12-point Times New Roman letter
And a blinking cursor on a bluish screen

When you say you need space
I don't feel the warm cloud
That barely radiates six feet
Emitting from a copper-coil mechanism
Of a bedroom heater on high

When you say you need space
I don't envision a parking lot
Of tidy lines graphed in yellow paint
Where a service van gets extra breathing room
And a lifted truck takes some too

When you say you need space
I get sucked into a vacuum
Of vast infinitesimal nothingness
And catapult beyond the reaches
Of sight, sound, taste and smell

When you say you need space
I only feel space
In all of its awesome, awful, awe
Space that is never ending
Space from which there is no return

"A Word Defined"

I won't go fishing for compliments
As an angler I've never been
But it sure is nice to have a fish
Fall in your lap now and then
I know that the adage would have you believe
Once taught, I could be self-sustaining
But my self-confidence is a boat with a hole
And my pond is shallow and draining
What's worse is, the fish you've presented me lately
Are all perfectly fine meaty breeds
Compliments to my brain and my character
They'd feed me for days if I needed
But the fish I desire are rarer
Small and slippery and sweet
Compliments that speak to the curve of my face
Would be a delectable treat
If you told me you woke with my name on your lips
And the desire to hold me in your arms
That you dreamt of my eyes, wide and blue
And my body was among my many charms
That'd be a feast that would nourish me
For innumerable days without end
But I'm neither a beauty nor a fisherman
I'm not gonna ask you to pretend
When we both know of other villagers
Who deserve those fish more than I
I won't go fishing for compliments
I'm not so hungry that I'll die

"I'm Not the Fisherman's Wife"

I overfilled the bathtub

In an attempt to get clarity
And calm frayed nerves
When I was already on the edge
Of a major mental breakdown

I overfilled the bathtub

While holding back tears
And trying to ground myself
To talk over the anxious demons
Playing racquetball in my brain

I overfilled the bathtub

By trying to find solace in water
And literally wash away
All the ugly, angry, filthy stress
In the best reset I know of

I overfilled the bathtub

(continued -->)

And in doing so —
My eyes followed suit
And my soul opened up
With the drain pull

I overfilled the bathtub

And when you ask me
Why I'm a sobbing mess
Crumpled in a heap
On the dirty bathroom floor

I overfilled the bathtub

Is the only response I have
And you think I'm crazy
And overdramatic
As you glance at the bone-dry porcelain

"I Overfilled the Bathtub"

From the moment I wake up
My thoughts flit to you
How you're feeling, what you're thinking
What's on your plan today to do
My body longs to hold you
Can almost sense you across the miles
I yearn to kiss your temple
And see that contented smile
My fingers twitch and nearly ache
With a need to trail your back
As if touching you is their purpose
They're the train and you're the track
You're flooding all my senses
Before I can even shake off dreams
So just know that my good morning text
Says way more than it seems

"Morning! 🐨"

Your hands spread love
In smooth, methodical strokes
Like a perfect even coating
Of butter on thick toast
Economy of motion
Is a wonderful ideal
But sweet deliberation
Has a delicious appeal
The way you hyperfocus
On a task with care
Is easily art in motion
Your personal attentive flair
Bleeds into everything you do
In intentionality you immerse
Being in the moment
Is your blessing — not a curse
There's no need to rush it
Just keep showing up
And take all the time you need
Spreading the love

"Take the Time to Do It Well"

My fingers are drawn to
The warmth of your skin
Like moths to flickering flame

To tiptoe across your arms
Gently slide down your back
And then up the way they came

My hand reaches out
Of its own accord
Like an animal that can't be tamed

In quiet moments
When they feel you need
A comfort only touch can name

A love language request
Unspoken but easily met
By fingers that feel the same

"Intuition of Fingertips"

You came inside me
And my God — the feeling
A rush, a crash, a low groan
Eyes rolled to the ceiling
You shutter, you mutter
A epitaph or a prayer
Is it supposed to be this good
Biology's not fair
You call me baby in a sigh
You moan, writhe and gasp
My heart contracts, my insides too
To hold you in its grasp
I'm memorizing the moment
Watching you settle back to stasis
Mmm, you came inside me
And it was the fucking greatest

"Yes, I Pinned This Moment Too"

I exhale
I wait
Sit still
And just be

That's where you'll find me

In days
In weeks
Or even years
I'm here
I'm yours

Each piece
A token taken
Each time
A little more

So I exhale
And wait
Be here
Be yours
Just be

And wait for you to find me

"Find Me"

Your words never lied to me
But your actions did
Or maybe I have that flipped around
Because one of them loved me
And the other one continually let me down
And I can't remember which one it was
Because there were arms that held me
And future possibilities spoken into existence
But there were withheld kisses and turned backs
And language that belittled and hurt
But never at the same time
So I never figured out which one was real
Maybe it was neither
Maybe it was both

"When Actions and Words Are Both Screaming,
It Doesn't Matter Which One's Louder"

Boy, why are you crying
And why do you come to me
When your shadow's unraveled
And starting to flee

I'd trade you a kiss
But you don't know what that means
So I'll give you a thimble
That's full of my dreams

You taught me to fly
And so I play house with you
But this game is just a game
That can never be true

Love shows up like a mother
When you've never had one
And breaks fairies' hearts
When all's said and done

Because Wendy leaves Neverland
To be home by sun up
And lost boys stay lost
Not knowing what they gave up

(continued -->)

Until Peter returns
To find dear Wendy grown
No longer a girl
That can get shadows sewn

Both find the moment
A bit bittersweet
And neither regrets
That they happened to meet

But Peter can't stay
And Wendy can't leave
And a fairy can't fix this
No matter how hard you believe

Boy, why are you crying
Is there more here at stake
Tell me how many Wendys
Is it going to take

Before you stop taking kisses
Give up bouncing off walls
And let something simple
Be the biggest adventure of all

"A Darling Dares to Dream"

I eat cheesecake at 2 a.m.
Having snuck back into the house
Still on the phone with you
But desperate to warm up my chilly bare toes
That meandered the dewy lawn in time with our conversation
My tired body scavenging for energy
Not sleep though — my heart forbids the very thought
No, cheesecake and giggles become my fuel
Perched on the counter
Letting your words wash down my sugar binge
I give up sleep and sensibility
And settle for bliss

"My Heart Is Seventeen and Doesn't Have a Bedtime"

I wake with the rising sun
On the coast she graces first
Twenty-five hundred miles
From where she'll set with you
But it's the same sun
In the same day
And I'm living this life
That's made better because you're in it
So, I greet the rising sun
While you still sleep
And tell her to shine down on you
And carry my love to you in her rays
Which she can bring you at the speed of light
Faster than text messages
Faster even than my voice on a call
Warming you in her light
And my love
During the day, she can hold us both
When we cannot hold each other
Even so, I'm grateful for these early moments
When it's just her and I
And I can whisper to her over my coffee
All the things I want her to tell you

"The Sun Takes a Message"

My body is rioting with memories
Of your hands glancing over my curves
Softly at my face, firmly at my waist
Tender and worshipful and teasing
Your mouth, my God, your mouth
Perfectly dancing with my own
(Was that choreographed by fate too?)
But then exploring with intuitive wayfinding
And always just the right combination
To have me floating just outside myself
Waiting to crash back in at your insistence
My skin feels electric and my soul is on fire
And I wake up with curses, praises, epithets
And your name on my lips
Because even though you're not here
My body can't forget

"My Skin as a Sensory Scrapbook"

I want a love like a late 90s country song
That sizzle Tim and Faith couldn't fake
I want high notes that Martina belted
And a line dance hook I can't shake
I want a love like a late 90s country song
Alan Jackson's half smile approved
Something Shania might've dance to
A story Randy Travis might have crooned
I want a love like a late 90s country song
Sung by Wynonna or Clint or Reba
Give me Trisha, Garth or Travis Tritt
Lonestar, Brooks & Dunn, Alabama
I want a love like a late 90s country song
Not the heartache or breakups or blues
But the sweet simple love I grew up on
I want a 90s country love song with you

"A 90s Country Love"

Parroted back reassurance
Doesn't make me feel better
Yes, it's what I want to hear
But not at my request
I honor your love language
And mindfully dole out
The human touch you crave
Gently grazing your arm
As you talk or we sit together
But when I ask for calming words
You bristle, sometimes snarl
Barking that it's not your job
To assuage my worries constantly
I'll own my anxiety, sure
But constantly meeting my unease
With unyielding silence
When I beg for words of affirmation
Or asking what I want you to say
Isn't fair
Isn't kind
Isn't love
Isn't going to work for me, babe

"Love as a Second Language"

The rain knows our story
She was the court stenographer
The documentarian with the camera at the ready
She was the ghostwriter penning our fate
(Is it biography? Memoir? Romance? Fairytale?)
The rain was there in all the moments
The non-player character in each scene
She never drove the plot or even spoke a line
But without her there'd be missing depth
A palpable void only she could fill
She was the crew on the stage, clothed in black
That set up the door for us to open
Ready to feed us a line in the quietest whisper
Give us a nudge at our cue
Because the rain knows our story
And she's not gonna let us miss a beat of it

"The Rain Knows Our Story"

Let me orbit you
So I don't hurtle away or too close
Perfectly balanced in your gravity
Let me be a satellite
And bask in your reflective glow
Spin slowly, steadily by your side
Let me be your moon
Waxing and waning in comfortable time
And gifting you only gentle tides
Let me orbit you

"I Don't Need to Be Your Sun"

There's a quiet space
In a wooded place
Where I watched the awe dance on your face
As we walked in the semi-dark

You lit up in your memories
And small, beautiful discoveries
Gave way to childlike reveries
From the moment we embarked

Slivered moon glistening high
Spiderwebbed branches in lavender sky
The song of a trickling creek bubbled by
And then my favorite part

You took my hand
And surveyed the land
And I began to truly understand
The depth of what's in your heart

The crunch of snow
Our voices low
The quiet ways that a love can grow
When you tend it from the start

"Exploring"

When you are sleepy
On the very edge of consciousness
You say the things you don't say all day
About loving me
About how my love affects you
About how you don't think you deserve it
Turn it around and call me crazy
For giving it to you so freely
When I know it's just you
Being self-critical again
Because my way of loving you
Looks different than yours for me
But one isn't better than the other
Nor is love about keeping score
So I just keep at it anyway
Despite the protests and comparisons
Touching you with soothing fingers
And soft lingering kisses on your back
Until your words quiet
And your brain quiets
And your body quiets
And you drift off to sleep
Because my love is powerful
And you don't have to earn it

"You Don't Have to Earn My Love"

Your face
A slice of moon
In stark relief
Against a bed
Of velvet stardust
Softly sighing
While my fingers
Dance along
Your back
A child skipping
In a wildflower meadow
More tender though
And reverent
An earthly goddess
Gifting a sky god
Endless tithes of faith
With waxing glow
You turn toward me
And lips connect
In the softest whisper
Like the summer sky
Paints a quiet kiss
When it tells the earth
Goodnight

"Goodnight, My Love"

You blast — go fast
Gulp down life before it's passed
Go big, try it all
Jump without looking
Enjoy the fall
Faster and faster — no brakes
Busy learning
If you make mistakes
It's cake — life is a game
Win or lose, it's all the same
So why not get a thrill
Live your fill
Really blast, both up and down hill
Even still — it's not greed to exceed
Your need for excitement and speed
But take heed before you bleed
Life isn't a race or a chase
Yes, you can make haste
But don't lay waste
To the things and the people
Who care — will always be there
In the wings, on a chair
Waiting for their chance to say
"Truth or Dare" — and implore
That you take a chance on the first
Before you burst
In your madcap dash to quench a thirst

(continued --›)

So deep and so real
You hardly know how you feel
Grip the wheel, make a deal
But give us a chance to appeal
Let them be the ones
To hold one foot to ground
Slow you down
Just long enough to look around
And give you a chance to see
The excitement to be
In a world where things
Can exist without frenzy
A moment of clarity
Is what you could gain
If you stopped the bullet train
And danced in the rain
My refrain — just this
Delivered with a kiss
When you are off blasting
Be aware what you'll miss

"Blaster Mode"

My love is a community garden
An open and uplifting zone
Where everyone's welcome to visit
Or take root and call it their home
My love's a community garden
With expansive and rich soil beds
Where seedlings are fiercely protected
Weary travelers can rest their heads
My love, like a community garden
Provides nourishment to those in need
There's room for the hardiest shade tree
And starting trays for the smallest seed
My love is a community garden
A rescue for pot-bound or diseased
Houseplants are welcome to unfurl themselves
Your hopelessness here can be eased
My love's a community garden
Tended by all who step up and come in
And choose to take part in our seasons
Wherever you want to begin

(continued -->)

My love is a community garden
Growing larger all of the time
Your love is garden too, I see
A kindred idea to mine
Our love is community gardens
That blossom into more love abounding
'Til the world is just lush and growing
And the effect will be truly astounding
Love is community gardens
Love is wildflowers that roam
It's orderly rows of vegetables
It's compost and clippings and loam
It's sharing the bounty of harvest
It's a trellis to support a weak vine
Love is a community garden
Welcome, with love, to mine

"Love Is a Community Garden"

I watch you fold yourself
Like paper
In half and in half
And in half
Folding back inside yourself
Getting smaller
You looked up how many times
A paper could be folded in half
Before it became impossible
And I'm watching you
Test the theory
Almost like a badge of honor
And I worry
That you'll let yourself disappear
Or hurt yourself
In a show of force
Against physics
You're meant to be origami
Not a tiny square

"The Art of Folding Paper"

Your head on my lap
Your eyes closed
We're comfortable
In this casual pose
Neuroscience chat
Playing on your phone
You're half asleep
I feel at home
Our fingers entwined
It's a simple night
No pretense or drama
It just feels right
Two on the couch
Relaxed and unstressed
This is my dream
I'm quick to confess
Your head on my lap
My hand on your face
If this isn't heaven
It's a close enough place

"Blissful"

You are a hurricane
And I am the sea
I'm giving you the power
You rain back down on me
You could be a little cloud
And storm yourself out
Without muss or fuss
Or much more than a pout
But instead I fuel you
Stir up tropical waves
If you didn't have me
Perhaps your moods would behave
If your personal weather
Had less reaching effects
You might feel more in control
Of where it directs
But how does the ocean
Say into the air
"I'm sorry, I love you —
But you shouldn't care"

(continued -->)

I just think that maybe
The pressure's too great
When you're met with an ocean
There's too much at stake
So you take in my water
Grow huge and start spinning
Perhaps it's a tempest
We were fated from the beginning
If I were calm, still waters
And you were soft, warm skies
Would the love still be there
Could passions still arise
'Cause with you as a hurricane
And I, formidable sea
How can we settle comfortably
And just simply be

"Tropical Depression"

You deserve love without conditions
That meets you where you are
That shows up for you regardless
When you're near or maybe far
A love that holds a space for you
Free of guilt, manipulation or rage
That lets you just be who you are
Doesn't keep you in a cage
You deserve unconditional love
That is present in a hundred tiny ways
A soft touch, a leant shoulder
A listening ear, some quiet praise
A cheerleader from the sidelines
A person to call on when things are rough
A love that tells you daily
You are special, you're enough
You deserve love that's undemanding
Love that never breaks or bends
Love you cannot push away
Love that never ends

"Unconditional Love Is a Basic Necessity"

"That's my girl," you said
As I rose and fell
Simultaneously
At your insistence
I came for you
But felt your love for me
In a way that was just giving
You wanted me to feel good
And praised me
Not for how it was for you
But for allowing myself
To just let go
Which is the best thing
You've ever given me

"Your Girl"

The thing I've discovered about feelings
Is that they can never truly be reciprocated
Because mine are mine
And yours are yours
And they're laden with
Years of experiences to filter through
Both shared and not
So while we can do our best
To listen, empathize and learn
Reflect, process and recreate
The best we can do is want to connect
And give grace when it doesn't look like we expect

"The Myth of Reciprocity"

I wish I had taken a picture
Of the way your face looked
In those moments when you'd stare
So full of real affinity and love
It shook me and took my breath away
Those deep looks that moved me
Because I could see you were moved too
I wish I had captured that gaze
Because I want to feel it again
The prickle of my skin under your eyes
The catch of my breath, battling my heart
Both racing to jump out of me
The depth of it that made falling feel like floating
And the question and answer that we distilled it to
Because "yeah?" and "yeah" covered it all

"You Know the Look I Mean"

Crisp air
Warm sun
The metronome of steps
Yours and mine
On city streets
But no city noise
Because all I can hear
Is your voice
And your heart
And your soul
And the unhurried steps
Yours and mine
As we walk
Arm in arm
Breathing in sunshine
And crisp air

"A Simple, Wonderful Moment"

Ignition is the moment
The flying sparks catch
And light a fire
Setting off a chain of events
Like a domino chain
Or a Rube Goldberg machine
Or the rush of two bodies together
But there is a split second
When the sparks are suspended
In their creation
Like that weightless shift
Before a fall in a rollercoaster
Like a change in a thriller's score
Like the parting of lips
And a unison gasp
The second that doesn't put the act in motion
But makes it feel like magic

"Click"

I don't have a single token
To hold in my hand
And make loving you
The only thing in my brain
I have a song you ruined
And a dress you love
A bracelet that matches one you don't wear
I have pictures that tell lies
And poems that tell hard truths
And I have your voice in my head
Saying all the things you can say
And none of the things you can't
But the first are growing fainter
And the latter are deafening
The things and places
I had assigned meaning to
Are not what I thought they were
And I have empty spaces in my day
That used to be spent with you
And all the nothingness
Begets more nothingness
And how do you purge
The things that don't exist

"If You'd Gifted Me a Trinket in All Our Time Together"

Your hand on my back
At 3 a.m.
I was asleep
And so were you
But somehow we found each other
In the turmoil of sheets
And mental barriers
Were you comforting me
Or seeking comfort yourself
Slipping into old habits
Or forging something new
Because I kind of like the feel
Of your hand on my back
At 3 a.m.
When I'm asleep
And so are you
And everything is calm and easy
A hand is just a hand
And it doesn't have to mean anything
But I can still feel glad
It felt safe landing there

"I Was Asleep, and So Were You"

Do you remember
The first time you kissed me
The not so silent
Rush of air you expelled
And the low mmm of satisfaction
When you pulled away
Eyes still closed
You said you could've
Kept kissing me all night
I wish you had
I wish you never stopped

"First Kiss Last"

You just want to be in love
Is what you tell me
Like I don't understand
The head-over-heels
Totally obsessed
Single mindedness
That comes with new love
Like I can't imagine
The desire to flood yourself in it
Or the way new love
Permeates your every thought
Like I'm not intimately familiar
With the way new love
Grabs you suddenly
And holds you hard
Like I'm not still there myself
Like a few months isn't still new
Like you don't see that I know
What it feels like to want to be in love
Or that I just want to be in love too

"I Want That Too"

You cannot get lost
Inside of my love
It isn't a confusing maze
But a meditative labyrinth
There are no dead ends
Or trick turns
You're safe here
My love is a practice in zen
An exercise in consciousness
And all the intricate twists therein
Are an infinite path that lead you
All the way through my heart
And back to yours
In an endless loop
That we are both the creators
And the idle travelers of
And within which
There is no beginning nor end
Relax within my love, dear
And give up charting a course
The labyrinth will lead you
Right back to where you have been

"My Love Is a Labyrinth"

I dreamt about you
Which is wild
Because I've never met you
I don't know
What your voice sounds like
The timbre of your laugh
The clean, cedary smell
Of your shirt against my face
Or if I'll really have
To get on my toes
To wrap my arms around your neck
It's all conjecture
My sleepy brain
Creating a plausible possibility
Or maybe
I was granted a glimpse
At some future encounter
Where you and I
Exist in the same space

"Flash Forward"

There are poems I don't share publicly
Little jagged, broken pieces of my soul
Raw open nerves that crackle like downed wires
Fledgling truths that would shrivel in the elements
I have unimaginable depths
There are poems that would make your skin itch
Heck, you'd probably crawl right out of it
And poems that would reduce you to tears
I have written poems about you
That will never, ever see the light of day
For fear that overexposure would bleed their colors right out

"Private vs. Public Poems"

And the castle started to crumble
After the king's guard took their leave
The moat lay dry and ashen
The drawbridge left open to siege
The once ever-creeping ivy
Dried and withered on the vine
The angel statue near the chapel
Seemed to weep, resigned
The formerly opulent banners
And gilded coat of arms
Have faded and gave way to dust
The stained glass has lost its charm
The epic mighty stonework
Where footfalls clicked and echoed daily
Lay cold and silent all around
No jester vamped around gaily
The throne room mocked of history
And held space for a once grand court
But now only reverberated emptiness
And gave silence as retort
Fairytales can fall apart
And somehow lose all of their power
When you stop believing in the magic
Even from the highest tower

"A Princess' Lament"

You gave me your tee shirt
As a token, a memento
Even asked if you could
In that sweet apologetic way
I've come to know as your signature
Telling me it still smells like you
Saying it's a favorite of yours
And insisting I have it
Despite my protests
You joked not to let another man take it
(As if I'd let that happen)
And speculated it could be a sleep shirt

I think I surprised us both
When I took off my tank top
And slipped into it immediately
Asserting that it was a 'right now' shirt
Smiling up at you flirtatiously
As the soft material fell around my shoulders
Feeling like your arms around me
And smelling like two magical days
I never want to forget

(continued -->)

Because now, you're gone
And I'm home in my lonely bed
Wearing your tee shirt
(Just as you predicted)
And a bittersweet smile
As I wonder how many times I can wear it
Before it stops smelling like you
How can I make the scent as indelible
As the other memories I'm going to carry
Of your hands in my hair
The whispered words 'every inch of you'
Echoing in my brain
The gentle kisses on my face
The feel of your skin under my fingers
And your arms around me
So tightly, so possessively, so appreciatively
That I'll never be the same

"A Forever Shirt"

I want to write about love
In all the old clichéd ways
Talk about breathless meet-cutes
Wanton, reckless abandon
Beating hearts and flushed faces
I want flowery language
Depicting soft kisses
Like dew on rose petals
And passionate lip locks
As torrents of crashing waves
I want to pen polaroids
Of hands finding other hands
Of hearts finding other hearts
Of heads finding gentle resting places
On strong chests or soft laps
I want to write about love
Until I repeat all the ways
Every other writer has tried to capture it
And I run out of words
But never inspiration

"To Write About Love"

I felt a shift
Like the ground moving under me
Or the wind changing
Heard Dick VanDyke
Whisper-sing about something brewing
In a terrible cockney accent
Somewhere in the back of my mind
As a shiver rolled
Up my back and into my brain
I tried to breathe into it
Or out of it maybe
But ended up choking on a sob
Because big changes
Mean giving things up
To make room for the new
And however great the things
On the horizon may be
Or how ready you are to release
Old energy to the ether
Endings are hard
And change comes
Like loose sand
Under unsteady feet
Ready to send you toppling

"On the Cusp of Change"

You blessed me with a curse
Because I guess I never knew
That I was missing anything
'Til I was missing you
You treated me so gently
Made me forget being alone
Now I'm aching for your presence
Constantly checking my phone
It's borderline obsessive
And obsession isn't cute
But to say that I was smitten
Would be pretty close to truth
How can I keep your interest
When we only barely met
How much can we build upon
Two days we can't forget
And do you even want to
Or did this spell just curse me
Because I'm already entangled
Do you want to set me free
Or do you want to try this
Explore a friendship across miles
Attempt to recreate the magic
That keeps me in wistful smiles
Because I'm ready to do it
See what happens next
Because I'm hoping and I'm betting
That you've been likewise hexed

"Spellbound"

Every woman needs a little black dress
You confirmed the sentiment
And lapped up the delicious vision of me
Clad in that skin-tight cliché
Turning me around and nodding appreciatively
You made me feel like a million dollars
In a dress I bought for less than a cup of coffee
Having tricked the system with an employee discount
And a clearance rack find
It was your money, and I could have spent more of it
But I'm a bargain hunter
And you must be too

Because a dress that cheap is disposable long before it's worn out
And so, it seems, was I

"Little Black Dress"

I know you wish
I wouldn't kiss and tell
You say you aren't ashamed
But who needs to know
That your body and mine
Crave one another
That my hands will find
Your back or waist or arm
As soon as you're in close proximity
Or that your mouth
Remembers the way I taste
And couldn't stop itself
From kissing me today
Or telling me you love me
Before you left my side
To remind us both
You'd come back soon
Why don't you want
Anyone else to know
Unless you're hiding from yourself
And the fact that being with me
Feels like coming home

"Homesick"

When your storm clouds spread
I sat with you in them
Until you were ready
To step back into the sun
And then I watched it
Bathe you in light
And celebrated that with you
We weathered your storms together
When my storm clouds came
You were on the other side of the street
Where the sun was still shining
And you could see a rainbow
But I couldn't find an umbrella
To make it to you safely
And you were too happy to want to get wet
But standing on the edge of my sadness
Was already getting you damp
So I ruined your rainbow either way

"The Weather in Central New York
Has Always Been Impossible to Forecast"

I'd cast a spell to keep you
But I know it wouldn't last
And if it did, I'd have regret
That you weren't holding fast
For reasons pure, romantic, true
At least your own volition
To make you stay would undermine
The very purpose of the mission
They say set free the things you love
And they'll come back to you
But freedom feels like letting go
And who knows if it's true
If you fly away with your next whim
And leave me here to pine
You'll fill up with new energies
And forget the draw of mine
The only choice I guess I have
Is cherish you while you're here
Release you from obligation
Likewise release my fear

"Casting Away Doubt"

I can't make your bed
Even when you show me how
You like things a very specific way
And that seems cute right now

I'm terrible with money
Too spendy, generous, unconcerned
I buy stuff that I can scarcely afford
While you focus on ways you can earn

You always pick what we watch
Like I don't have any measurable taste
And though I like what you've shown me
Our interests aren't evenly paced

I'm messy, lazy, have lots of baggage
You're snobby, neurotic and driven
If opposites attract is a common rule
For us, it must be a given

Lucky for us we're both aware
That a relationship isn't the sum of its parts
It's respect and integrity and commitment
And holding open space in our hearts

"Paula Abdul Wasn't Wrong"

You tilted my chin up
And kissed me goodbye
So quickly —
I couldn't tell if it was because
You thought it was a bad idea
And wished you could talk yourself out of it
Or because you psyched yourself up
And didn't want to lose your nerve
Or maybe —
The impulse caught you by surprise
And our lips connected
Before you even realized
You were kissing me
Or that you wanted to

"So Quickly"

I used to think I wanted a cowboy
Someone wild and worldly to whisk me away
A man whose sideways smile stirred excitement
And promised adventure at every turn
But I forgot that Willie warned me
How hard a cowboy is to hold
That a man like that is full of pride
Is listless, aimless and often afflicted
With a wanderlust and restless soul
They hang their hats in temporary stands
And don't let dust settle on their boots
Cowboys break hearts without even meaning to
And sometimes those hearts are even their own

"Mamas, Don't Let Your Lovers Turn Out to Be Cowboys"

I peppered your back
With a million tiny kisses
Instead of the usual
Soft and hypnotic
Fingers soothing muscle
I calmed your body
With the gentle metronome
Of puckered lips meeting warm skin
Down your spine
Across your shoulders
Up your neck
And back again
Felt your tension melt
Heard you murmur appreciations
And then sighs
And finally the quiet, even breaths
That signaled your fall
Into sleep
And out of stress
So I can rest
After a handful more kisses
Knowing you'll be okay
At least for a few resting hours

"A Twist on Our Bedtime Ritual"

Something unexpected happened
As I made myself indispensable
Wove my essence into the fabric of your life
Became your partner
In every sense of the word
Promised to be your foundation
And grew to be your home
Between wanting to be the tether
That kept you from spinning out
And the safe space
You could always land
Something unexpected happened
When I wanted my voice
To be one you could always trust
And my gentle touch
To be the comfort and strength
You came to rely on and crave
Something unexpected happened
Because somewhere in the process
Of becoming each of these things to you
You became them to me

"I Don't Know Why It Surprised Me"

Of the hundreds of times
You've said "I love you"
I knew this one was different

There was weight to it
Its own gravitational pull
And a pregnant pause

I let it hang there between us
Like an aerialist who let go of the trapeze
And seems to float, waiting

I saw the intensity in your eyes
Heard your brain cogs turning, churning
With what you were trying to convey

"Is there something else?"
I asked, inviting you to be clear
To me, to yourself

And you laugh, release your breath
Still surprised after all this time
That I can read you like a book

"Yeah," you say, and nod
"I wanted it to mean something"
And I let you fill me in

"Commitment"

If I could spin a fairytale life
Out of the raw material I have
I'd find a happy ending
Down a yet untrodden path
No one can see the future
But it's worth the leap of faith
To commit to the unexpected
To stop lying in wait
I believe in promises
Made in good faith speculation
Even if they end up broken
It's still worth the declaration
Lean in to what brings happiness
Walk without a safety net
If not for the risk of falling
You'll guarantee regret

"Jump"

Someone asked me the other day
If I believe in love at first sight
And I laughed
Not the derisive laugh of disbelief
But the knowing laugh

A reminiscent giggle at those first interactions
A warm chuckle at the intensity with which it bloomed
A hearty chortle at our shared inability to quantify it
Or even really speak it at first
A head-shaking guffaw at others attempt to understand

Do I believe in love at first sight?
The thought makes me laugh still
The saddest little sigh of a laugh
Because I do believe in it
But I'm not sure believing in it is enough

"I Laughed, Did You?"

I have memorized every speck
Freckle, mole and mark on your back
Down your arms and on your chest
You're a living star map
You're a galaxy, a universe
And my fingers trace constellations
I create an entire new astrology
To base all my wild whims upon
And let your body chart a course
For a future yet unknown

"Checking My Horoscope"

A once in a lifetime love
Is what you called it this morning
Then proceeded further
With letting your mouth
Tumble out with your big feelings
And opened up my eyes
To how much I truly mean to you
And effectively silenced
The meanest parts of my brain
That still believed
I was just a dalliance
And this was just a fun way
For you to spend a few months

"You Are My World, and I Am Your Home"

A rope swing
And a lazy creek
And a cool little gully
Bathed in green
Contained us
Coddled us
Became a magic glen
Where our effervescent laughter
Filled the humid air
As kids doggy-paddled
And a puppy dipped toes
Where stress melted away
Leaving space for calm
And so much love
Where we locked eyes
And smiled simply
When we felt the power
And pinned this moment
For future inspiration

"A Dip in the Local Waterhole"

George offered Mary the moon
But I'd rather gift you the sun
You shine better under its warmth
You seem to have more fun
No one checked your care tag
When they planted you here in the shade
Your leaves are going limp and lifeless
Your colors are starting to fade
No amount of nutritive soil uptake
Can overwrite your basic need
For the energy of photosynthesis
That only sunlight can feed
So I can keep giving you TLC
And focus on strengthening your roots
But if your leaves really wither here
My efforts will be moot
It's time to build a giant lasso
And rope the sun for you
I want to see you thriving
So it's the least that I can do

"Plant in Full, Direct Sunlight"

If home is where your heart is
And your heart's a vagabond
Where would I send a letter
If I needed to correspond
If your heart is like Odysseus
Gathering experience along your way
Then I can be Penelope
And sit at the loom all day
Until Calypso lets you go again
If it's the will of the Gods to be
Until Circe's done her time as well
And finally sets you free
If you can tempt yourself with siren song
Square off with dangers thrilling
I can wait and weave away
And keep my life fulfilling
I can hold down all of Ithaca
And keep things with me unchanged
And I'll hold enough of your heart here
That a feeling of home can be arranged
You can have decade-long adventures
But never fear Poseidon's rage
If your story is an epic poem
And you let me be the stage

"Homecoming"

I'm moved to write sonnets about you
Ink out many poetic love notes
Build worlds of words in celebration
Of the things on which I dote
But when I get a bit garrulous
Going on in a complimentary way
It tends to make you squeamish
I watch you tuck yourself away
I can't stop finding you beautiful
I can't quell my need to admire
The amazing human that I love
Whose mind and body I desire
        So here's an imperfect sonnet, written for you
        Entreating that you get comfortable with the rest too

"An Attempted Sonnet:
Learn to Take My Gushy Compliments"

I dreamt you said
All the things you feel
But cannot always
Put words to
Emotions you show
In millions of tiny ways
But sometimes fall short
Of telling me
Hearing them in my dream
Melted me
And I woke up more in love
Than yesterday
Or the day before
But on waking
My brain turned analytical
And tarnished the vision
Sneered a vile thought —
Are they really his emotions
Or the ones you dream he'd have

"A Dream Disrupted"

I'm exceedingly good
In stressful situations
Childhood trauma having prepared me
To be quiet, helpful and stay out of the way
But also be right there to lend a hand
Don't make any suggestions
But anticipate needed action and take it
I can stay calm
While you slam, or curse, or fret, or rage
And go on like nothing ever happened
When it all blows over
Damaged little girls
Make really good partners

"An Unpretty Revelation to Have in a Crisis"

Surplus happiness
Love abounding
My cup overflows
The effects are astounding
My life's leveled up
Because you are in it
So when I say I love you
Know that I mean it
From the depths of my soul
From the corners of my heart
Reaching into my past
From the absolute start
And into the future
As far as I can see
You are the magic
Pouring into me

"A Love Poem at Midnight"

A sigh
I hear it in my sleep
And still my breath, my heart
Listening hard
A sigh
Again, and you shift
You're restless
Stressed
Pained maybe
I stir
Enough to let you know
That I'm here
Next to you
I don't want to fuss over you
But I want you to know
That I'm here
A sigh
Another shift
I roll toward you
Wait
Will you reach out if you need comfort?
My fingers itch
To soothe
To love
I can't resist
My hands and lips on you
And gentle murmurs
Then —
A sigh

"I'm Here"

You read to me in bed
A classic dystopian romance
    Am I the only one who considers 1984 a romance?
Lying next to me
Transporting me to other worlds
With your soft, unhurried voice
In a clear, confident style
    Is it funny that I find even your voice sexy?
I'm awash in the moment
Flooded with the imagery
And engrossed in the plot
But still acutely aware of you
Gently turning pages next to me
    Did Julia ever feel like this about Winston?
This simple pastime
The deliciousness of shared text
And the intellectual stimulation
Paired with our cozy closeness
Feels like true romance
And a special type of quiet intimacy

"Reading for Pleasure"

I love you not out of habit
Or because it feels nice
Or due to obligations
Or because of our physical relationship
Or in some Pavlovian response to your feelings for me
I love you on purpose
Because I choose to
Because I truly like you as a person
As a friend and a fellow human
And loving you is what I want to do
And doing so is a gift to myself
I love you unconditionally
Knowing that you love me too
But not even needing that to be true
Because loving you is a choice I make again and again
And again

"Love on Purpose"

A "sepia tone memory"
Is the beautiful poetic moniker
You attributed to the passage of time
When the earth paused
The movie score in our heads swelled
And people around us looked up
Feeling the change in the atmosphere
Moved to tears by the shutter scope view
We gave them a look into

And the way you put it was romantic and tender
But for me, it'll always be bursting with color

"A Kodachrome Memory"

Half asleep
With closed eyes
And unencumbered brain
You reach across the bed
And find me
Fingertips to warm skin
And we both melt into it
You aren't one to name your emotions
As each one parades through you
But I like to imagine
That in that melty moment
You feel happy and contented
Of course loved as well
Something akin to blessed
And maybe a little wonder-filled
Just as I do

"First Contact"

I'm impulsive
Sometimes it makes me exciting
I'm the girl with an easy smile
A friendly chatterbox
That brings strangers into social circles
And creates adventures out of possibility
Sometimes it makes me flaky
I'm the girl who rearranges plans
Texts erratically and never answers calls
Says 'yes' to overlapping events
And forgets who she told which story to
Sometimes it makes me passionate
I'm the girl who buys unexpected gifts
A grab-your-hand-in-excitement storyteller
Who believes in love at first sight
And doesn't balk at public displays of affection
Sometimes it makes me irritating
I'm the girl who talks too loudly
A grocery aisle karaoke singer
Who plans overly complicated theme parties
And tends to lean a little too competitive
Yes, I'm impulsive
In complicated and beautiful ways
But I can't seem to rein it in
So I hope you find it more beautiful
Than complicated
And love me in all my impulsive craziness

"Impulsiveness"

I hold spaces specifically
To protect your peace
I lose time asleep or elsewhere
To be by your side whenever you need me
And give up beautiful possibilities
To preserve your comfort
And harden my heart
To the lesser dreams and wishes
I have to give up so I can keep you

But I would make the same choices
I'd release all sorts of things
I'd clear the difficult spaces
I'd let go of many small joys
I'd transform a thousand times
To retain the biggest dream
And honor the commitment I make
Each morning when I wake up
And choose loving you
Above the other things

In all the considerations
I make for you
Walking away is a thought
I never ever entertain

"Not Even a Consideration"

I heard you
When you told me
You needed me
Holding my hand
And watching me
Struggle with being unwell
I heard your words
I heard the meaning too
And when I joked
About not getting so attached
You could have laughed
But instead you persisted
Reminded me of your commitment
And squeezed my hand again
And I accepted that
With a content smile
When what I should have said
Was I need you too

"I Heard You"

In my head
I broke up with you
Fifty different ways
And each one
Tears me to shreds
So in real life
I recommit to you
Fifty different ways
And each one
Chips at my ability
To be without you
'Til I'm not sure
What is worse
Being without you
But gutted
And devastated
Or being with you
But codependent
And clingy
When both options
Suck for everyone
And neither option
Is who I'm committed
To being

"I'm Not Broken, I'm Not Needy"

You would read to me in bed
Until I fell asleep to your voice
And I never knew intimacy like that

We would sit and work
Side by side in relative silence
And I never knew intimacy like that

You would share a podcast
Eager to talk to me about it
And I never knew intimacy like that

You took me to new places
And delighted in sharing new experiences
And I never knew intimacy like that

But then you left
And that all went with you
And I never knew loneliness like this

"Intimacies"

People talk of moving mountains
To better reach their loved ones far away
I wish I could move just one here
To keep you closer every day
It's not that I take it personally
Your wish to run back to your home
There's just no way I could go with you
And without you, I feel alone
My heart breaks for what you're missing
I ache to give it all to you
Your friends, the pace, the liveliness
The safety of what's more familiar too
I wish I knew how to ease your pain
Give you everything you ever need
Is it just your own loneliness or nostalgia
Wanting to live life at a different speed
Are you remembering through rose-colored lens
Or am I holding you captive here
And if I set you free right now
Would you forever disappear
I love you too much to try to keep you
And too much to just let you leave
So today I wish fervently to move mountains
And gain a little time to breathe

"If Colorado Were in My Backyard"

I listen to you breathe
Across an expanse of real estate
That only a king mattress can afford
Close enough to hear you
Reach out and touch you
But far enough away
That bumping knees seem less accidental
And more like a subtle reminder
That I'm here across the plain
Inviting you to touch me back
And close the growing gap

"A Thought From My Side of the Bed"

There's a weight to reality
That imagination can use as a tether
And we all know flights of fancy
Are light as a feather
Dreamers are known to
Go where the wind takes us
Thank goodness for realists
Who know where to stake us
It takes all kinds of people
To keep our world spinning
I can't help that I've been
A dreamer from the beginning
And where the dreamer drags you
You know you will thank her
So you keep us grounded
I'll let you be my anchor

"Give and Take"

Two lovers enter an antique store
To kill a little time and just peruse
Both have an eye for character
But purse strings that can't be loosed
"Do you think this sweater will fit"
"Can a dress like this be altered at all"
"Honey, am I crazy if I buy a spoon"
"35% off everything in this vendor's stall"
"Whoa, check out this drafting table"
"This teapot is begging to come home with me"
"Keep your eyes peeled for ashtrays"
"Babe, can you hold my treasures while I pee"
Two lovers enter an antique store
And maybe buy a small couple pieces
But time spent picking at things from the past
Is how their love for each other increases

"Antiquities & Affection"

I counted the steps
Because I wanted to remember
How we got here
And how to get back

I carved out space
In my ever-crowded brain
To pin the moment
When everything turned

I dropped breadcrumbs
But forgot this was wonderland
And nothing makes sense
When you're upside down

But I also forgot the important thing
That you are here with me
So I'm not really lost
If I keep holding on to you

"Point the Way"

I wanted to be the girl in your bed
If you came home early
I didn't want to miss a single second
That I could be in your arms
So last night after checking your things
I just stayed
In your empty apartment
In your empty bed
I curled up, missing you
And slept
The best sleep I've had
In as many days as you've been gone
Breathing in your scent
Breathing in your space
Aching to be close to you
And taking what I could get

"I Slept Alone in Your Bed Last Night"

If I said your name in an audible gasp
While touching myself all alone
Would you hear it in your brain
Would it make you pick up the phone
If I writhed on my bed in ecstasy
While imagining your hands on my skin
Would your fingers tingle across the miles
Would you want to invite me in
If I hurtle toward physical rapture
With wanton reckless self-love
Would you know that it's you I'm imagining
Would you tell me you want me to come

"Double Entendre"

I think back to our first days
Our magnet period
Where we were drawn to one another
Intoxicated with each other's words
When life felt lived in earnest
Nights were spent contemplating physics
And soaking up every moment
Not wanting to sleep for losing time to talk
Our tired days were passed dizzyingly
Counting down each second 'til we reunited
And learning each other's bodies
Was an act of reverence and wonder
It's not that I want to go back
There is magic still now
In our easy companionability
And a true sense of partnership
I still feel intoxicated when you talk
And, my God, how I worship your body
Yet still some quiet mornings
I find myself wistful and misty
For those early days of eager electricity

"Magnet Days"

Reading a novel in bed
I felt the mattress shift
As you rolled toward me
My fingers casually settled
On the warm skin of your back
As if they belonged there
And traced the familiar landscape
In leisurely paths
Stopping regularly to turn the pages
But immediately returning to you
And their true calling
Until you rolled again
This time curling around me
And your hands started
Some idle exploration of their own
Making reading nearly impossible
So, when I dropped my book
And turned toward you as well
You said something about being distracting
I murmured back noncommittally
And kissed you hard
Because reading was the distraction
And this was the goal all along

"There's a Book on the Bedside Table"

My love shows up as
Running jokes and uncontained giggles
Homemade meals
And blonde hair on your clothes
My love shows up as
Passing along my coffee addiction
Off-key pop song serenades
And hand holding in the car
My love shows up as
Meaningful, lengthy conversations
Long hugs and forehead kisses
And constant cheerleading of your dreams
My love shows up as
New books popping up on your shelves
Reminders on the fridge
And quiet companionship from across the couch
My love shows up as
Soft fingertips on your back
A gifted painting in a frame
And roughly a dozen poems a month

"My Love Language"

I got drunk and took your wineglass
Right out of your hand
To kiss you
Affectionately
Assertively
It was a bold move on my part
Not something I'd normally do

You warned me when I came over
That you weren't good company
Low energy
Sleepy
Sick
But I pushed because I'm a fixer
And I thought I could cheer you up

I had good news of my own
Came in with excitement on my lips
Opened the door
Brimming
Beaming
Only to be confronted with storm clouds
And pain on your face

(continued --›)

I immediately switched to caretaker mode
Blanketed you in my healing touch
Listened to your worries
Sighs
Sadness
And when you opened a bottle of wine
We settled together into comfortable calm

But I changed the energy when I kissed you
You shrank and gently told me no
And I collapsed
Dizzying
Drunkenly
Into my own negative self-talk
And spiraled stormily into myself

I kissed you for me rather than for you
And that's where I made the mistake
And I blamed it on the wine
Stupidly
Selfishly
Because I wanted to clear your clouds
But now I have a matching set

"The Catchability of Storm Clouds"

When we parted ways
All those weeks ago
I gave you my necklace
As a token, a totem
A symbol of my affection
A worry stone you could carry
On hard days or sad days
Or times when you just needed
Something to hold
Knowing full well
There was a possibility
I'd never see it again
But today from far away
You sent me a picture of it
Doing its job perfectly
Wound around your fingers
And nestled in your palm
And I never thought I'd miss
A cheap piece of jewelry
I had bought for myself
But I'll be damned if I didn't think
Necklace, come home to me
And bring the man you're holding
Back to me too

"Bound by a Tiny Silver Chain"

I'm a woman of magic
I believe in the unbelievable
And savor the unexplained

You are a man of science
Researching and learning
And making sense of the nonsensical

When you talk of quantum particles
Crazy gaps in space and time
It stirs something familiar in my soul

Maybe that's your magic
The sexiest thing about you
Your brilliant genius brain

And maybe my attraction
Is believing that it's magic
While you expand my knowledge

And maybe your attraction
Is the scientific process of teaching
And growing and learning together

What if science and magic
Are just two sides of the same coin
And we're creating the common language

"We Create a Common Reality"

"You're my favorite person right now forever"
You said in one breath without punctuation
And I spent the whole next day
Trying to diagram the sentence
Did you intend to put a comma between the qualifiers
As if to say that both are true
And may even be progressive
Or did you mentally strike through the first
And the second was corrective
Had you paused or used a bit of inflection
Would I have heard a question in each
Like you somehow didn't know if one or either was true
Or is my brain just chasing geese
And you said it breathlessly because it fell off your tongue
Punctuationless and real
Because if I stop thinking so hard
Trying to make extraneous meaning
I'd look at you and say just as swiftly
"You're my favorite person right now forever too"

"Unedited Declaration"

Eyes brim, eyes fill,
Tears drip, tears spill,
Heart pangs, heart break,
Heart rips, heart ache,
Hold out, hold down,
Slipping smile, slipping crown,
Broken promise, broken heart,
Fall in love, fall apart

"A Sad, Short Poem"

There's a list
Deep in my brain
Of things I'm good at
Things I'm getting right
And things I'm proud of
And most of the time
That list includes
Being your partner
But lately I realize
That I made you promises
I'm not keeping
And in spreading myself thin
You aren't getting enough
Sometimes none of me at all
But you never complain
Just keep loving me
Bringing me coffee
Celebrating my experiences
And personifying compersion
Like the larger-than-life lover
You just continue to be
While I take you for granted
And love you selfishly
Because even as I write this
I lie to myself

(continued -->)

About fair not always being equal
And perpetuate the fallacy
Of time as enough to hold a bond
When in truth
I see a possible reality in which
I foolishly let you slip away
Or worse
Watch you starve and shrivel
Desperate for crumbs
Of the affection
I generously dole out
But forget to whom
I dedicated the original recipe

"I Stop to Evaluate What I May Be Overlooking"

I wore a short skirt
Too much makeup
And a loud headache
Thinking one might balance
The other two
Like gold nail polish
Could mend fences
Or men's sandals
Would somehow
Soften the blow
I brought you coffee
How you like it
And scarfed down a donut
In the car
So you wouldn't see
My fatal flaws
Or know I'm also human
Also broken
Also flailing wildly
Faking every move
And pretending it means
Something
Anything
Other than the nothing
We agreed on

"Maybe If I'd Worn Jeans,
 It Would Have Been Different"

I'm a lighthouse in a storm
And I'm the lightkeeper too
I'm shining and I'm burning
And I'm yearning for you
I'm the changing of the bulbs
I'm the constant nightly watch
I'm the waiting and the praying
I'm the space that time forgot
I'm the crashing of the waves
That mock and rock the other boats
I'm the greater purpose
That keeps my faith afloat
I'm the buoys in the bay
I'm the waiting port-of-call
I'm the steady stalwart lighthouse
If I'm anything at all

"Lighthouse"

Sometimes my mouth says all the right things
But my heart still breaks
And I can't make it understand good sense
The stuff that reason is made of
Is impermeable to the feelings
That I'm overcome by
You make a good argument
That feelings are just something we are at the effect of
But dammit if they don't fully consume me sometimes
Because I'm just a meat sack
Making meaning out of nothing
And sometimes that nothing is your words
And the meaning cuts me like a knife

"I Cry While You Sleep"

Brazenly
With bright eyes
And upturned mouth
I kiss you
Because I can't imagine
Waiting another minute
To have your body
As close to mine as possible
And my lips
Telling you how I feel
More clearly
Than my words ever could

"A Hello Kiss"

Your body is a miracle
Your brain is a work of art
Your soul is a revelation
I'm in love with every part
Where you see flaws or imperfections
I see character and beauty
To give you a better mirror for yourself
Is my honor and my duty
You're too close to the masterpiece
You only see the rough paint strokes
Step back with me and see the wonder
You project to other folks
Darling, you're a vision
You are wonderfully, dazzlingly you
If you could see what I see
You would just enjoy the view

"Pep Talk"

Freshly ground coffee
What a simple pleasure
But it's those little acts of service
That make me feel treasured
You even top it off for me
Because you know I like it hot
Give me the last pour
From the freshly brewed pot
You wanted to make sure I was cared for
Before you send me on my way
I never have had a cup of coffee yet
That has so made my day

"Morning Coffee"

The electric hum of your body
Your last exhale of battle-weary breath
Syncopated tapping of idle fingers on cool skin
The echoes of soft kisses and bolder kisses
Wet kisses, lazy kisses, sleepy kisses
All of the multiple millions of kisses
Whispered wantings and quieter regrets
Are the background track that plays
To the memories I keep rewatching
Bittersweet and beautiful melodies
Begging to be sampled and remixed
A new song for a new era

"Soundtrack"

If I could talk to your lovers past
And ask one question of them all
I'd ask if they still loved you
Then immediately feel small
Because I know already that they'd say
Without any hesitation
Again and again resounding yeses
There'd be no equivocation
So why bother to ask then
If I know what their answer would be
I guess I'm steeling myself
For when that question is asked of me
When five or ten years down the road
You've moved on to some new adventure
And the current keeper of your affection
Asks me of our past debenture
I'll look her squarely in the eye
After a tender weighty glance at you
And smile my most dazzling smile
And profess that it is true
To love you is to love you always
To know your love is transforming
To see you share love with anyone
Is enduringly heartwarming
If I could talk to your lovers past
Perhaps the question I should sub
Is will they hold a place for me
In their special love-filled club

"Exclusive Club Membership"

I kissed you for the last time
Five minutes into the new year
Not knowing that 2023 had started
Until we were already in it

My lips brushed yours then
As they had hundreds of times
Not knowing that 2022 had ended
And something else was ending too

It was a perfunctory kiss
Insofar as how new years are celebrated
But like everything else recently
It is laden with meaning in recollection

I kissed you for the last time
Both knowingly and unknowingly
Straddling my lips across the chasm
Of a calendar flip and a line in the sand

"A Kiss at 12:05 a.m. on January 1st, 2023"

I curl toward you
Wait for you to mirror me
Become two parentheses
With a meaningful thought
Just for us tucked between
Let the narrative all around
Cover us like a weighted blanket
Bask in the coziness
Of the bracketed meaning
That compacts and distills
As we close the gap between us
Coming together at the end of a sentence
And letting the punctuation
Fall to the outside

"The Only Meaning Worth Making (Love)"

Every time I hear Stevie plaintively croon
Maybe asking Lindsey but begging the moon
"Can I handle the seasons of my life?"
I'm gutted and broken, my chest gets tight
Was it the snow or the loneliness reflecting
Do mountains crumble or are they protecting
When we look around, with eyes clouded by tears
Can the child inside rise above our worst fears
Or once there's a crack, even a hesitation
Is a landslide a guaranteed demonstration
Of just how delicate it all can be
And did Stevie want answers or is that just me
Because after the landslide buries us deep
We can sort promises broken from those we can keep
Accept ending seasons, accept endless tides
Accept that the hard things are part of the ride
Give up finding meaning in the truth that you fell
Because I'm getting older and bolder as well

 "I've Been Afraid of Changing"

Sometimes the poet
With open heart but shut eyes
Builds universes with her words
That expand and rise
Envelope her loved ones
Drown out their voices
With no bad intentions
She stifles their choices
In expressing their feelings
They keep coming up lacking
How does one measure up
Without poetic backing
When she tells them of love
She paints giant murals
Each feeling she writes
Explodes into plurals
Then she sits and she waits
For some reciprocation
And they flounder for words
Worthy of her vocation
Little do they know
That her words have left room
For heartfelt wishes
That don't need to loom
Don't build her word castles
Inspire them instead
Simple honest declarations
Are all that need to be said

"To Gift Words to a Poet"

Brynn Ellen is a dreamer, wisher, mom, coffee addict and writer from Central New York. She has been writing poems since she was a child — her middle school haiku, "Freedom," still hangs in the upstairs hallway of her parents' farmhouse. While majoring in education and English at SUNY Oswego, one of Brynn's poems was published in The Great Lake Review (2008).

Brynn enjoys music, reading, performing (she's a founding member of one of Syracuse's longest-running improv comedy teams!) and cooking. She especially loves spending time with her two children — mostly getting her butt kicked at Mario Party or Settlers of Catan. If she's not at home, she is probably sitting under a waterfall, driving around while blasting 80s pop music or lost in an antique store.

Poems About You is her first collection of poetry.

Website: brynnellenpoet.squarespace.com
Instagram: @brynnellen_poet

www.ingramcontent.com/pod-product-compliance
Lightning Source LLC
Chambersburg PA
CBHW070719130626
46553CB00005B/2067